CONTEMPORARY'S

CHOICES
AN ESL LIFESKILLS SERIES FOR ADULTS
IN GOOD HEALTH

CONTEMPORARY'S

CHOICES
AN ESL LIFESKILLS SERIES FOR ADULTS
IN GOOD HEALTH

ELIZABETH CLAIRE

Senior Editor
Julie Landau

Consultants
Lenore Balliro
Adult Literacy Resource Institute
Boston, Massachusetts

Terrence J. Bray
Hacienda La Puente Unified School District
Hacienda Heights, California

CONTEMPORARY
BOOKS
CHICAGO

Library of Congress Cataloging-in-Publication Data

Claire, Elizabeth.
   In good health / Elizabeth Claire.
      p. cm. — (Choices, an ESL lifeskills series)
   Includes index.
   ISBN 0-8092-4048-3 (pbk.)
    1. English language— Textbooks for foreign speakers.   2. Life
skills—Problems, exercises, etc.   3. Health—Problems, exercises,
etc. 4. Readers—Health.   I. Title   II. Series: Choices (Chicago,
Ill.)
PE1128.C589   1991
428.6'4—dc20   91-14416
                                          CIP

Choices: An ESL Lifeskills Series for Adults was developed for Contemporary Books
by **Quest Editorial Development, Inc.**

This book is dedicated to Jim, Nadine, Jamie, and the newcomer.

Published by Contemporary Books, Inc.
180 North Michigan Avenue, Chicago, Illinois 60601
Manufactured in the United States of America
International Standard Book Number: 0-8092-4048-3

Published simultaneously in Canada by
Fitzhenry & Whiteside
195 Allstate Parkway
Valleywood Business Park
Markham, Ontario L3R 4T8
Canada

Editorial Director
Caren Van Slyke

Editorial
Craig Bolt
Robin O'Connor
Tim Phillips
Charlotte Ullman
Marietta Urban

Editorial Production Manager
Norma Fioretti

Production Editor
Marina Micari

Cover Design
Lois Stein

Illustrator
Gary Undercuffler

Cover photograph © C.C. Cain

■ ■ ■ ■ ■ ■ Contents

■■■■■ To the Student

Welcome to *In Good Health*!

In Good Health is part of Contemporary's ***Choices: An ESL Lifeskills Series for Adults.***

The purpose of this book is to give you information about getting health care and staying healthy in the U.S. *In Good Health* will also give you the language skills you need to use that information.

You already know how to get health care in your native country. *In Good Health* encourages you to compare the way you do things in your native country with the way you do things in the United States.

In Good Health offers valuable information about:

- reading medicine labels
- making appointments with the doctor
- asking questions about medical treatment
- understanding insurance policies
- dealing with government programs
- getting emergency care
- preparing for a birth

and many other health choices in the U.S.

We hope you enjoy *In Good Health*.

■ ■ ■ ■ ■ To the Teacher

Level

Choices: An ESL Lifeskills Series for Adults is designed for ESL students who are at the intermediate level. ***Choices*** will help students acquire the lifeskills competencies, language skills, and cultural information they need to make effective choices in the U.S.

Rationale

In Good Health provides a student-centered approach to language learning. It offers detailed information about health choices in the U.S. while providing opportunities for cultural comparison and teaching practical language skills. The ***Choices*** series features natural language that adult students can put to immediate use in their daily lives.

Format

In Good Health contains a *Tips for Teachers* section, twelve chapters, four review units, and an appendix. The review units are interactive information-gap exercises that appear after every three chapters, incorporating content from those chapters. The authors acknowledge Judith Winn-Bell Olsen and Richard C. Yorkey for inspiration in these exercises.

> For step-by-step information on how to use this book and for additional classroom activities, see ***Choices Teacher's Guide 1***.

Tips for Teachers

Everyone from the beginning teacher to the experienced professional can benefit from teaching suggestions. Textbooks can be used in many different ways, and what follows are notes on the purpose of the sections of *In Good Health* and how to use them.

The **Before You Listen** section prepares students for the dialogue by encouraging them to discuss the picture that illustrates it. Ask students to predict what they think will happen in the dialogue. This is a good time for you to assess how much the students know about the topic. If you want to teach key words before students listen to the dialogue, consult the **Words to Know** section.

There are a number of ways to present the **Dialogue**. It is helpful to act out the dialogue, doing something to indicate that you are portraying different people talking. For example, you may want to use different voices or change positions as you change roles. If the resources are available, you may wish to record the dialogue ahead of time. If you do this, make sure each character is vocally distinct, so that students know who is talking.

Discuss the dialogue, using the **Talking It Over** questions as a guide. Ask students if they have had experiences similar to the situation in the dialogue.

Assign different groups of students to different roles corresponding to characters in the dialogue. Have them repeat their roles after you. Have students practice the dialogue in pairs or groups. Ask for volunteers to perform the dialogue for the class.

Words to Know presents vocabulary that students need to know in order to understand the dialogue. The blank lines allow students to personalize the text by adding their own words to the vocabulary list. Encourage students to guess the meaning of vocabulary through the context and to refer back to the picture.

Another Way to Say It offers alternatives for some of the idiomatic expressions that are introduced in the dialogue. Have students read the dialogue again, inserting the new expressions. The blank lines in this section allow students to personalize the text by adding their own words to the vocabulary list.

Talking It Over should foster discussion about the situation presented in the dialogue and invite students to talk about how their own experiences relate to the situation. The questions in this section range from simple comprehension to application of the information to students' lives.

In **Working Together**, a role-play activity, students create conversations and put to use the language they have just learned. You may want to write the sample conversation on the board and ask students what they think should come next. Write their ideas on the board. After students have written the conversation as a class, have them practice it in pairs or groups and ask for volunteers to role-play it for the class. Then, have students create individual conversations based on relevant experiences.

Real Talk shows students how speakers of American English really talk. For that reason, it's important not to overarticulate when you present this section.

Putting It Together presents grammar in context. It focuses on one useful structure that appears in the dialogue. There is a short presentation of the structure and then a contextual exercise. This is followed by the opportunity to use the structure in meaningful, real-life responses.

In the **Read and Think** sections, students are asked to guess the meanings of underlined words. The content reading on this page provides information that students can put to use immediately. The **Read and Think** page is not always a reading passage. It often comprises real examples of the kinds of reading materials that people have to deal with every day, such as leases, warranties, phone bills, bank statements, and school and medical forms.

In Your Community offers students an opportunity to explore the community resources available to them. They can do this individually or in pairs or groups. You may also want to take students to a community-based organization during class time, invite a speaker to the classroom, or bring in realia such as the classified section of the newspaper.

Figuring Out the U.S. features an intimate look at one aspect of U.S. culture. Students are encouraged to circle any words in the passage they don't understand and to try to guess their meanings from the context.

Your Turn gives the students the chance to compare life here with life in their native countries and opens up avenues to all kinds of choices. Depending on the proficiency level of your students, the writing activity may range from a simple list to a paragraph expressing an opinion.

1 I Was Sick, but I'm Fine Now

Before You Listen

1. Who are the people in the picture? What are they waiting for?
2. Who is walking with a cane? Why?
3. What do you think the people are talking about?
4. Do you ride the bus to work or school?
5. Do you often see the same people? What do you talk about with them?

■ ■ ■ ■ ■ I Was Sick, but I'm Fine Now

Listen carefully to the dialogue.

Mike: Hi, Pavel. How are you?

Pavel: I was sick last week. I had a cold, but I'm fine now. How are you?

Mike: Just great.

Pavel: How's your mom? I heard that she was quite ill.

Mike: Yes, she had a very high fever. She's much better now, thank you. She's up and around and her spirits have improved.

Pavel: I'm glad to hear that. Tell her I said hello.
(*Luz arrives.*)

Luz: Mike! How are you doing?

Mike: So-so. I can't complain. How have you been, Luz?

Luz: I'm OK. But Carlos hasn't been well.

Mike: I'm sorry to hear that. What's the matter?

Luz: He worries too much. I think it's making him sick. His stomach always hurts him. He can't eat.

Pavel: I hope he feels better soon.

Luz: Thank you.

Words to Know

a cold	improved	stomach hurts
ill	worries	feels better
a fever	making him sick	soon

_____   _____   _____

Another Way to Say It

How are you doing?	....	How are you?
		How do you feel?
so-so	....	not good but not bad
I can't complain.	....	I'm fine.
up and around	....	well enough to get out of bed

_____ .... _____

■■■■■ Talking It Over

Discuss the following questions in pairs or groups.

1. Is Pavel sick now?
2. What did he have?
3. Who had a high fever?
4. How is she feeling now?
5. What's the matter with Carlos?
6. Do you get sick when you worry? What happens?
7. In the U.S., is it polite to ask about another person's health? What kinds of questions do people ask?
8. Have you or someone in your family been in a U.S. hospital? For what reason? How long did you (*he* or *she*) stay? What was it like?

Working Together

Practice these polite responses to health statements:

I'm sorry to hear that.
I'm glad to hear that.
I hope you (*he* or *she*) feel(*s*) better soon.

Work with your classmates and teacher to finish the following conversation. Then practice with a partner. Next, talk about the health of people in your family.

Person A: My brother is very sick.
Person B: What's the matter?

Real Talk

Many English words end with an *s*. Listen to your teacher say these words:

she's   worries   it hurts   feels

Notice that the sound is either "s" or "z."

■■■■■ Putting It Together

> **Yes/No Questions**
>
> I **exercise** five days a week.
>
> I **don't exercise** on Saturday or Sunday.
>
> Do you exercise every day?   Yes, I do.
>
> No, I don't.

Practice A

1. Read the following sentences. If the sentence is true about you, check *yes*. If it is not true, check *no*.

   I exercise every day.   ☐ yes ☐ no
   I eat well every day.   ☐ yes ☐ no
   I drink a lot of water every day.   ☐ yes ☐ no
   I rest every day.   ☐ yes ☐ no
   I worry.   ☐ yes ☐ no
   I smoke.   ☐ yes ☐ no
   I sleep well every night.   ☐ yes ☐ no
   I take vitamins every day.   ☐ yes ☐ no

2. How many sentences did you check *no*? _____ Use those to write negative sentences on a separate sheet of paper. Follow the example.

   Example: *I don't eat well every day.*

Practice B

Interview five students to complete the following chart. Use this model:

Person A: Do you exercise every day?
Person B: Yes, I do.
          or: No, I don't.

Name	Exercise	Sleep well	Take vitamins	Eat well
Chung			✔	✔

■■■■■ Read and Think

Read the following passage and try to guess the meanings of the under-lined words. Rephrase each paragraph. Then answer the questions.

The Common Cold

The common cold is the most <u>frequent</u> cause of absence from work. The usual <u>symptoms</u> are a <u>runny</u> <u>nose</u>, sneezing, coughing, muscle aches, and sometimes a <u>sore</u> <u>throat</u>.

A cold is <u>spread</u> from one person to another through tiny <u>droplets</u> in the air from sneezing or coughing. You can also <u>catch</u> <u>a</u> <u>cold</u> through kissing or handling tissues or towels that have been used by a person with a cold. People cover their mouths with their hands when they cough or sneeze, so hand <u>contact</u>, such as shaking hands, spreads colds too.

There are many different <u>viruses</u> that can cause cold symptoms. For this reason, doctors cannot make a <u>vaccine</u> to prevent a cold.

1. What are the usual symptoms of a cold?
2. What are two ways that colds are spread from one person to another?
3. Why can't doctors make a vaccine to prevent colds?
4. How many colds did you have last year?
5. What were the symptoms of your last cold? How long did it last?
6. What do you think this means: "Feed a fever; starve a cold"?
7. What do Americans say when a person sneezes? What do you say in your native country?

In Your Community

Find out the information individually or in groups and share it with the class.

1. Interview an employer at a store, factory, or office. Ask how many days of work are lost each month because of illness. Ask what the most frequent cause of absence is. Report to the class.
2. Look at a Fahrenheit thermometer and a centigrade thermometer. What are the highs and lows on each scale? What is normal body temperature on each scale? What is a mild fever? What is a dangerous fever? Why should you not wash a thermometer in hot water?

■ ■ ■ ■ ■ ■ Figuring Out the U.S.

As you read the passage below, circle the words you don't understand and try to guess their meanings.

Health Trends

Many Americans are very health conscious. They are careful about what they eat. They try to eat foods that are low in fat, sugar, cholesterol, and salt. They take vitamins to supplement their diets.

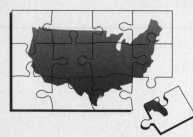

Exercising has become very popular, especially among people who do not get much exercise at their jobs. Most exercises are good for the heart and the lungs. Many people jog, swim, work out, or participate in other sports. Gyms, health clubs, and parks are popular places to exercise.

There is now a national campaign against smoking. Since people can get ill from breathing cigarette smoke, there are no-smoking areas in restaurants and public places. The labels on cigarette packages warn against the dangers of smoking. However, some smokers find it difficult to quit, and other smokers don't want to quit.

Your Turn

Discuss the questions.

1. What are some ways to improve health?
2. Do you think most Americans are health conscious? Why or why not?
3. Are people in your native country concerned about their health? In what ways?
4. In your native country, what foods do people eat in order to stay healthy?
5. What kinds of exercise do people get in your native country? What do you think is the best way to exercise?
6. Do many people in your native country smoke? Do you smoke? (Have you ever smoked? Did you try to stop? What happened when you tried to stop? How did you stop?)

> *Choose one of the questions and write about it.*

What Can You Recommend?

Before You Listen

1. What kind of store do you see in the picture?
2. What do you see in the window of the store? What else do you think the store sells?
3. What do you think the two men are saying?
4. Where else can you buy toothpaste and medicine?
5. What medicines do people use in your native country? Do they buy the medicine or make it themselves?

■■■■■ What Can You Recommend?

Listen carefully to the dialogue.

Carlos: Mike, can you recommend something for an upset stomach?

Mike: When I have an upset stomach, I take Peptaid.

Carlos: Is it a pill? I can't swallow pills.

Mike: It's a liquid.

Carlos: Oh, good. Where can I buy it?

Mike: In a drug store or a supermarket.

_____

(Carlos enters the drug store.)

Carlos: Excuse me. Do you have Peptaid?

Pharmacist: It's on the middle shelf in aisle three, near the front of the store.

Carlos: I've never used it before. How much should I take?

Pharmacist: The dosage is on the back of the bottle. Take two tablespoons every four hours.

Carlos: Does it have side effects?

Pharmacist: No, I don't think so. I'll check the label for you.

Words to Know

recommend	swallow	tablespoons
upset stomach	liquid	side effects
take (medicine)	aisle	label
pill	dosage	
_____	_____	_____

Another Way to Say It

pharmacist .... druggist

pharmacy .... drug store

_____ .... _____

■■■■■ Talking It Over

Discuss the following questions in pairs or groups.

1. What does Carlos ask Mike?
2. What does Mike take when he has an upset stomach?
3. Where can Carlos buy Peptaid?
4. What is the dosage on the Peptaid bottle?
5. What do you take when you have an upset stomach?
6. In the U.S., what do people eat or drink when they have upset stomachs? What do they eat or drink in your native country?

Working Together

Person A asks Person B to recommend a medicine to take or something to do (rest, drink tea, etc.) for each problem. Person B responds. Then switch roles.

1. A: Can you recommend something for a *sore throat*?
   B: When I have a *sore throat*, I _____.
2. A: . . . a stuffy nose?
   B: _____.
3. A: . . . a headache?
   B: _____.
4. A: . . . chapped lips?
   B: _____.
5. A: . . . a burn?
   B: _____.
6. A: . . . a cut?
   B: _____.

Real Talk

In English there are many words that begin with the letters *ph* and are pronounced with the sound "f." Listen to your teacher and then say the following words:

pharmacy   **ph**ysician   **ph**ysical

■ ■ ■ ■ ■ Putting It Together

> **Commands**
>
> **Take** Peptaid for an upset stomach.
> **Don't take** Peptaid for a headache.

Practice A

Work with a partner. One person gives advice about what to do. The other person gives advice about what not to do. Follow the example below.

1. **A:** Use Chaplip for chapped lips.
   B: <u>Don't use</u> _____ Chaplip for sunburn.

2. **B:** Buy packages that are sealed.
   A: _____ packages with broken seals.

3. **A:** Ask the druggist about side effects.
   B: _____ your neighbor about side effects.

4. **B:** Take this medicine before bedtime.
   A: _____.

5. **A:** See a doctor.
   B: _____.

6. **B:** Eat healthy food.
   A: _____.

7. **A:** Drink lots of water.
   B: _____.

8. **B:** Exercise three to five times a week.
   A: _____.

Practice B

Your son or daughter has an upset stomach. On a separate sheet of paper, write two things your child should do and two things your child shouldn't do for an upset stomach.

Example: *Stay in bed.*
Don't eat too much.

■■■■■ Read and Think

Read the labels below and underline the words you don't know. As you read, try to guess the meanings from the way they are used. Rephrase each instruction. Then answer the questions below.

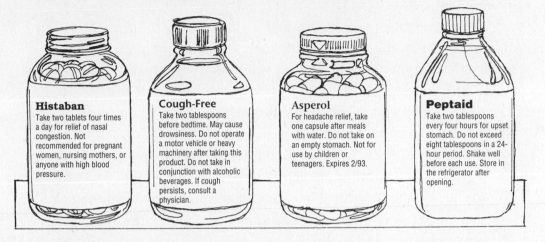

Histaban
Take two tablets four times a day for relief of nasal congestion. Not recommended for pregnant women, nursing mothers, or anyone with high blood pressure.

Cough-Free
Take two tablespoons before bedtime. May cause drowsiness. Do not operate a motor vehicle or heavy machinery after taking this product. Do not take in conjunction with alcoholic beverages. If cough persists, consult a physician.

Asperol
For headache relief, take one capsule after meals with water. Do not take on an empty stomach. Not for use by children or teenagers. Expires 2/93.

Peptaid
Take two tablespoons every four hours for upset stomach. Do not exceed eight tablespoons in a 24-hour period. Shake well before each use. Store in the refrigerator after opening.

1. Which medicine is for a cough? a headache? a stuffy nose? an upset stomach?
2. What is the dosage for Histaban?
3. Mike's wife Olga is pregnant. Should she use Histaban?
4. What time of day is best for using Cough-Free? Why?
5. Should Luz drive a car after taking Cough-Free?
6. Carlos took a dose of Peptaid at 8 A.M., 12 P.M., 4 P.M., and 8 P.M. Can he take another dose at 12 A.M.?
7. Where should Carlos keep the Peptaid after he opens the bottle?
8. Should Mike give Asperol to his four-year-old daughter?
9. Mike has had a cough for a week. Should he take Cough-Free?
10. Pavel drank wine at a party at 9 P.M. Should he take Cough-Free at bedtime?

In Your Community

Divide into groups. Each group will research one of these questions and share its answers with the class.

1. Visit a pharmacy. How many different over-the-counter cough medicines can you find? Ask the pharmacist what prescription cough medicines do that over-the-counter ones cannot do. Ask why a prescription from a doctor is needed for those drugs.
2. Watch some TV commercials for medicines. Make a list of the brand names and what they are remedies for. Compare with the lists that other students make. What medicines are advertised the most? What effect do you think TV commercials have on people's use of drugs?

■■■■■ Figuring Out the U.S.

As you read the following passage, circle the words you don't know and try to guess their meanings.

Natural Remedies

Many Americans take over-the-counter medicines for minor medical problems such as a cough or a stuffy nose. Other people prefer natural remedies. They might gargle with salt water for a sore throat. For a cold, 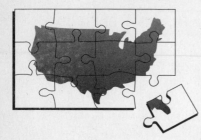 some people drink hot tea with honey, or they eat chicken soup. Some people take certain vitamins and herbs for specific problems.

Some people prefer natural remedies because over-the-counter medicines have side effects. For instance, some allergy medicines make you sleepy. And medication can cover up serious illness by relieving the symptoms.

Natural remedies are usually cheaper. Also, their effect on the body is not as strong. Many natural remedies are passed down in families from grandmothers and mothers.

Your Turn

Discuss the questions.

1. What natural remedies are common in your native country? in the U.S.?
2. When you have a minor illness or pain, what do you try first, a natural remedy or an over-the-counter medication? How do you choose? Tell about a time when you had to make this choice.
3. How do you decide whether to see a doctor?
4. Do you know anyone who has taken a natural remedy for a serious medical problem? What happened?

> *Choose one of the questions and write about it.*

Before You Listen

1. Who is Carlos talking to on the telephone?
2. What do you think he is saying?
3. How many patients are in the waiting room?
4. What problems do they have?

■■■■■ Have You Been to Our Office?

Listen carefully to the dialogue.

Receptionist: Dr. Alamo's office.

Carlos: Hello. I want to make an appointment with Dr. Alamo.

Receptionist: What is your name, please?

Carlos: Carlos Lopez.

Receptionist: Have you been to our office before?

Carlos: No, I haven't.

Receptionist: What time do you want to come in?

Carlos: I work in the daytime. Can I get an appointment at night?

Receptionist: Our evening hours are six to nine. How is next Thursday at seven?

Carlos: Can I come sooner? I have a terrible pain in my stomach.

Receptionist: Yes, I think we can squeeze you in. Is eight o'clock tomorrow all right?

Carlos: OK, that's fine.

Receptionist: Very good. We'll see you tomorrow night at eight o'clock.

Carlos: Where are you located?

Receptionist: We're at 42 Main Street, near the corner of Madison.

Words to Know

receptionist	evening hours	pain
appointment	terrible	corner
_____	_____	_____

Another Way to Say It

How is next Tuesday? .... Can you come (do it) next Tuesday?

squeeze you in .... find time for you

Where are you located? .... Can you give me directions?

_____ .... _____

■■■■■ Talking It Over

Discuss the following questions in pairs or groups.

1. Why did Carlos call the doctor?
2. Did Carlos like the first time for an appointment? Why not?
3. What time is his appointment?
4. Why did Carlos ask for directions?
5. Where is Doctor Alamo's office?
6. Why is it necessary to make an appointment with some doctors?
7. Do you need an appointment with your doctor?
8. Have you made any appointments on the phone? Have you ever misunderstood the time or day? What happened?

Working Together

Work with a partner to set up an appointment. One student will be a receptionist, and the other one will be a new patient. Make up additional questions.

1. What is your name, please?
2. Would you spell that for me?
3. What is the problem?
4. What's your telephone number?
5. What time do you want to come to the office?
6. Have you been to our office before?
7. Do you need directions?

Real Talk

When the receptionist at Dr. Alamo's office makes an appointment with Carlos, she repeats the time:

Thank you, Mr. Lopez. We'll see you tomorrow night at eight o'clock.

It is very easy to make mistakes with numbers, so it is always helpful to repeat numbers and to ask others to repeat them.

Example: *Would you repeat that telephone number for me, please?*

Wh-Questions: When

| Can | you | come to our office? |
| When can | you | come to our office? |

To ask a question about time, put *when* in front of the question.

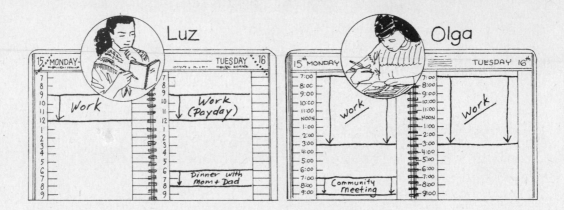

Work with a partner. Look at the appointment books. Person A asks the questions, and Person B answers them. Then switch roles.

1. **A:** Can Olga go to the doctor on Tuesday morning?
   B: No.
   A: When <u>can she go to the doctor</u>_____?
   B: _____.

2. **A:** Can Luz go to the doctor on Monday morning?
   B: No.
   A: When_____?
   B: _____.

3. **A:** Can Olga meet Luz for dinner on Tuesday?
   B: No.
   A: _____?
   B: _____.

4. **A:** Will Luz get paid on Monday?
   B: No.
   A: _____?
   B: _____.

▪▪▪▪▪ Read and Think

As you read this form, underline the words that you don't understand and discuss them with the class. Then fill in the form with your own health history.

Health Form
Lorenzo Alamo, M.D.
42 Main Street
Newtown, N.J.

1. Name _____
2. Address _____
3. City, State, Zip _____
4. Date of birth mo. ___ day____ yr. ___ Present age _____
5. Place of birth _____
6. Sex M___ F___ Married____ Single ____ Divorced____
7. Number of children_____ Ages _____
8. Please check (√) any of these illnesses you may have or have had in the past.

[ ] AIDS	[ ] diabetes	[ ] kidney stones
[ ] allergy	[ ] dizziness	[ ] measles
[ ] appendicitis	[ ] epilepsy	[ ] mumps
[ ] arthritis	[ ] German measles	[ ] parasites
[ ] asthma	(rubella)	[ ] pneumonia
[ ] bronchitis	[ ] heart disease	[ ] tumor
[ ] cancer	[ ] hepatitis	[ ] ulcer
[ ] chicken pox	[ ] high blood pressure	

9. Have you had major surgery? yes___ no___
   For what?_____ year _____
10. Are you taking any medications now? yes___ no___
11. Are you allergic to penicillin? yes___ no___
    Are you allergic to any other antibiotics or medications? yes___ no___
12. Have you had a large weight gain or loss in the past year? yes___ no___

In Your Community

Work individually or in pairs to answer the questions.

1. In your native language, make lists of the illnesses you and members of your family have had. Find out and write down the English equivalents (talk to a doctor who speaks your native language and English, or use a good bilingual dictionary). Keep this list and take it with you when you go to any English-speaking health professional.

2. Visit a doctor's office or a clinic near you and ask the receptionist for a health-history form. Share it with the class.

3. Bring in a local telephone book and look at the Yellow Pages. Find the listing for *Physicians and Doctors*. How many different specialists are listed? Do doctors advertise in your native country? How?

■■■■■ Figuring Out the U.S.

As you read the passage below, circle the words you don't understand and try to guess their meanings.

Finding a Doctor

In the United States, you can see a doctor in many places. For instance, you can go to private practitioners' offices and clinics. The cost of services and the care you receive are different in each place.

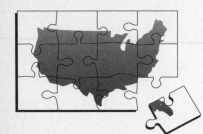

- **Private practitioners:** These doctors have their own offices and see the same patients regularly. They get to know their patients and keep a record of their health histories. These doctors do checkups and treat mild medical problems. For more serious problems, they recommend specialists.
- **Clinics:** In a clinic, a group of doctors works together. Patients may not see the same doctor each visit.

But, if you go to a clinic regularly, the clinic keeps a record of your health history. Some clinics are set up for poor patients, so the costs are not very high. Sometimes costs are based on a sliding scale—that is, patients pay according to their own incomes. In many clinics, you don't need an appointment. Clinics are located in hospitals or in neighborhoods.

Your Turn

Discuss the following questions.

1. What kind of doctor or healer did you go to in your native country?
2. Do you regularly go to a doctor or healer now?
3. How did you find your doctor?
4. Are you satisfied with the health care you receive now?
5. How do you know if a doctor is good or not? What would you do if a doctor you went to gave bad advice?
6. Other medical options include women's health centers, community health centers, group practices, and hospital emergency rooms. Have you been to any of these? If so, describe your visit.

> *Choose one of the questions and write about it.*

Person A

Work with a partner. Look at this page only, and your partner will look at page 20 only.

You hurt your back when you went bowling last Thursday. It is now 12 noon on Monday, March 13. You are on your lunch break at work. You are calling your chiropractor, Dr. Becker, to make an appointment. You work Monday through Friday from 9 A.M.–5 P.M. This is your calendar.

M A R C H

Sunday	Monday	Tuesday	Wednesday	Thursday	Friday	Saturday
				Bowling 7-10 pm		Movies 7 pm
				2	3	4
			1			
	ESL Class 7-9 pm			Bowling 7-10 pm		
5	6	7	8	9	10	11
	ESL Class 7-9 pm	School: Parent Conference 7-8 pm		Bowling 7-10 pm		
12	13	14	15	16	17	18
	ESL Class 7-9 pm			Bowling 7-10 pm	Dinner with friends 6 pm	
19	20	21	22	23	24	25
	ESL Class 7-9 pm			Bowling 7-10 pm		
26	27	28	29	30	31	

Person B

Work with a partner. Look at this page only, and your partner will look at page 19 only.

You are a receptionist for Dr. Becker, a chiropractor. Below is your appointment book for the week of March 13–17.

It is 12 noon on Monday, March 13. A patient calls you for an appointment. Schedule an appointment with the patient for this week.

March	13 Monday	14 Tuesday	15 Wednesday	16 Thursday	17 Friday
10:00	Miller		Ross		Sepsie
10:15	Kay		Rosen		Basakowski
10:30	Blank				
10:45					Di Bella
11:00	Gomez		Wheeler		Baffa
11:15	Sand		Cucci		Cook
11:30	Peña		Intovri		
11:45	Cruz		Arodopolous		
12:00	Nestor				
12:15					
12:30	Wing		Sita		
12:45	Bush				
1:00	Kerin		Longo		Lay
1:15	O'Donnell		Fort		
1:30			Kassler		
1:45					Rhodes
2:00					
2:15					
2:30	Hill				Lee
2:45	Lee		Scheraga		Gelman
3:00	Nguyen		Yedlin		
3:15					
3:30					Yi
3:45	Yamada				Voytec
6:00	Yang				
6:15	Garcia				
6:30	Wong				
6:45	Mato				
7:00	Simms				
7:15	Pasto				
7:30	Crespo				
7:45	Ossi				
8:00	Martin				
8:15	Gerder				
8:30					
8:45	Banks				

4 Show Me Where the Pain Is

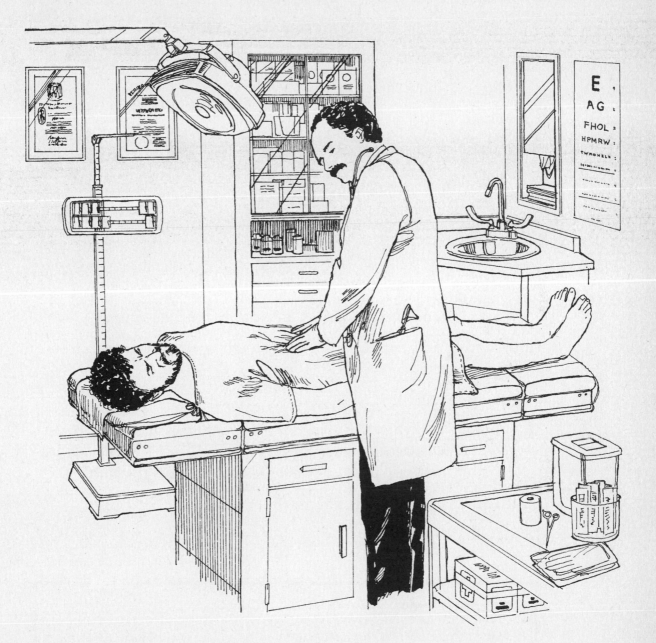

Before You Listen

1. Where is Carlos?
2. What is he wearing?
3. Who is examining him?
4. What do you think Carlos told the doctor?
5. What questions do you think the doctor will ask Carlos?

■ ■ ■ ■ ■ Show Me Where the Pain Is

Listen carefully to the dialogue.

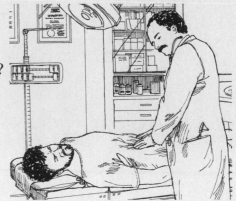

Dr. Alamo: What seems to be the problem?

Carlos: I have a pain in my stomach.

Dr. Alamo: How long have you had this pain?

Carlos: About three months.

Dr. Alamo: Show me where the pain is.

Carlos: It's here.
(He puts his hand on the center of his abdomen.)

Dr. Alamo: Does the pain come and go, or do you always have it?

Carlos: It comes and goes.

Dr. Alamo: Did you take anything for it?

Carlos: I took Peptaid. Sometimes it helped and sometimes it didn't.

Dr. Alamo: Well, let's see. Open your mouth, stick out your tongue, and say "ah."

Carlos: Ahh.

Dr. Alamo: Very good. I'm going to check your lungs and heart. Then I'll take your blood pressure. *(He does that.)* Lie down on this table. *(He presses on Carlos's abdomen.)* Does this hurt?

Carlos: Ouch. Yes. That hurts a lot.

Dr. Alamo: Hmmmmm.

Words to Know

how long	tongue	blood pressure
abdomen	lungs	
_____	_____	_____

Another Way to Say It

What seems to be the problem? .... What's wrong?

I have a pain in my _____. .... My ____ hurts.

I have a sore ____.

_____ .... _____

■■■■■ Talking It Over

Discuss the questions in pairs or groups.

1. How long has Carlos had the pain?
2. Where is the pain?
3. Does the pain come and go, or does he always have it?
4. Name five things that Dr. Alamo checks.
5. For what kinds of problems do people go to a doctor?
6. Did you ever go to a doctor with a problem?
7. What questions did the doctor ask you?
8. What did he or she check?

Working Together

Work with your classmates and teacher to complete the following conversation. Write down the conversation. Then practice with a partner.

Doctor: What seems to be the problem?
Patient: _____.

Doctor: How long have you had this problem?
Patient: _____.

Doctor: What other symptoms do you have?
Patient: _____.

Doctor: Did you take anything for this problem?
Patient: _____.

Real Talk

Many English words begin with groups of consonants called *blends*. Some consonant blends can be difficult for new speakers of English. Listen to your teacher and then say the following words:

problem	pressure	improve	pretty
stick	stomach	store	street

Questions and Answers in the Past

Question:	**Did** you **take** anything for it?
Answer (affirmative):	Yes, I **took** Peptaid.
Answer (negative):	No, I **didn't take** anything.

Here are some verbs with irregular forms in the past tense:

take/took	buy/bought	cost/cost
have/had	feel/felt	find/found
go/went	read/read	shake/shook

Work with a partner. Person A asks questions and Person B plays the role of a patient who was sick. Then switch roles.

1. **A:** When did you feel sick?

   B: <u>I felt sick last night</u>   .

2. **A:** Did you have a fever?

   B: _____.

3. **A:** Did you take any medicine?

   B: _____.

4. **A:** Did you read the directions?

   B: _____.

5. **A:** Did you shake the bottle?

   B: _____.

6. **A:** How much medicine did you take?

   B: _____.

7. **A:** Did you go to a doctor?

   B: _____.

8. **A:** _____?

   B: _____.

■■■■■ Read and Think

As you read the chart below, underline the words you don't know and try to guess their meanings. Then answer the questions that follow.

A Home Medical Guide

The following chart contains information that you would find in a home medical guide.

Medical Problem	Possible Symptoms	Comments
Appendicitis	Severe pain in the abdomen, nausea, vomiting, fever	Is usually an emergency. See a doctor right away.
Bronchitis	Coughing, wheezing, shortness of breath, mucus in the lungs	May be caused by a virus or by breathing cigarette smoke.
German measles (rubella)	Rash, fever, enlarged lymph glands in the neck	Dangerous for pregnant women; very contagious.
Pneumonia	Headaches, fever, muscle pain, sore throat, coughing	May be very severe; may last two or three weeks.

1. What are the symptoms of bronchitis?
2. Name other illnesses not listed on the chart. What are the symptoms?
3. Do you think it is good to know the names of symptoms? Why or why not?
4. How can you learn about different medical problems and symptoms?
5. How can you learn about preventing diseases?

In Your Community

Find out the information individually or in groups and share it with the class.

1. Call a community center or hospital near you. Ask if it offers health lectures. Find out if it has printed materials in your native language.
2. Find a medical advice column in a newspaper. Read one letter and the doctor's response. Discuss with the class whether or not you should rely on this advice to someone else.
3. Choose four medical problems that you want to learn about. Look through a home medical guide or encyclopedia to get information. Make a chart like the one on this page.

■■■■■ Figuring Out the U.S.

As you read the passage below, circle the words you don't understand and try to guess their meanings.

Participating in Health Care

For many years, it was said that "the doctor knows best." The doctor was the expert. The patient accepted the doctor's advice without question. But some Americans became dissatisfied with the health care they were receiving. They began to learn more about medicine, and they wanted to participate in their own health care.

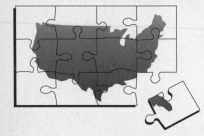

If *you* want to be more involved in your health care, here are some things you can do:

• **Prepare for any visit to a doctor.** Think about your medical problem. When did it start? What are the symptoms? What home remedies or medicines did you try? Write down this information and bring it with you. This will help the doctor make a diagnosis.

• **Ask questions during the visit.** For example, you could ask: What is the exact term for my medical problem? What is the cause? What kinds of treatment are possible? How much will each one cost? When will I start to feel better? Am I contagious?

• **Get a second opinion.** If your doctor recommends surgery or an expensive treatment, go to another doctor and get his or her opinion. You will have more information to make a decision about your treatment.

Your Turn

Discuss the questions.

1. Do you think it's a good idea to prepare in advance for a visit to a doctor or healer? to ask questions? to get a second opinion?
2. In your native country, did you do any of these things?
3. Compare a visit to the doctor in the U.S. with a visit to a doctor or healer in your native country. What's the same? What's different?

> *Choose one of the questions and write about it.*

We'll Have to Run Some Tests

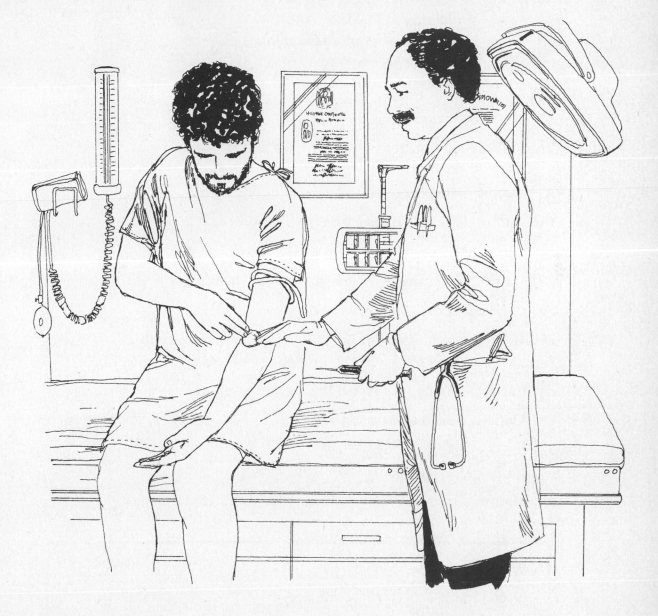

Before You Listen

1. What test do you think Carlos had?
2. Have you ever had a blood test? Did it hurt?
3. Do you think the doctor will do any other tests? Why or why not?
4. Will they cost a lot? Why do you think so?

■■■■■ We'll Have to Run Some Tests

Listen carefully to the dialogue.

Dr. Alamo: We'll have to run some tests on you. First, I'm going to take a blood sample. Make a fist. *(Dr. Alamo draws Carlos's blood from a vein in his inner arm.)* OK. Hold this cotton here.

Carlos: OK.

Dr. Alamo: I'd like to get an X-ray of your stomach and intestines.

Carlos: Are you going to do that right now?

Dr. Alamo: No, you'll have to go to a radiologist.

Carlos: What will the X-ray show?

Dr. Alamo: We can see if there are any obstructions.

Carlos: What's an obstruction?

Dr. Alamo: Your intestines are like a very long tube. Anything that stops food from passing through the tube is an obstruction.

Carlos: Thanks for explaining. Are there any risks to the test?

Dr. Alamo: Good question. It's not safe to have too many X-rays. But there is very little risk from this small amount of radiation.

Carlos: Is this going to cost a lot?

Dr. Alamo: You'll have to discuss the fee with the radiologist.

Words to Know

blood sample	intestines	risks
fist	radiologist	radiation
cotton	obstruction	fee
X-ray		

_____ _____ _____

Another Way to Say It

to run a test .... to perform or do a test
to take a blood sample .... to draw blood

_____ .... _____

■■■■■■ Talking It Over

Discuss the questions in pairs or groups.

1. What test did Dr. Alamo perform?
2. What other test did he recommend?
3. What will the second test show?
4. Carlos doesn't know what an *obstruction* is. What does he do?
5. Can Dr. Alamo take X-rays in his office? Where will Carlos have to go?
6. Are there risks to the X-rays?
7. Is the test going to cost a lot?
8. What other kinds of medical tests are there?
9. Have you ever had X-rays or other tests?
10. How can you find out if a test is safe?

Working Together

Work with your classmates and teacher to finish the conversation below.
Practice with a partner. Then write your conversation.

Doctor: I have to run some tests.
Patient: What tests?

Real Talk

The names of many specialists in the medical field have five or six
syllables. Listen to your teacher say the following words. Mark where the
stress is. Follow the example.

radiologist   gynecologist   dermatologist

cardiologist   pediatrician   neurologist

chiropractor   ophthalmologist   obstetrician

■■■■■ Putting It Together

Future with *Going To*

I	**am**	going to take a blood sample.
He/she	**is**	going to have X-rays.
It	**is** not	going to hurt much.
You/we/they	**are**	going to get better.
Are	you	going to do any tests?
Is	he/she	going to get worse?
Is	it	going to cost a lot?

Practice A

Work with a partner. Person A asks the question and Person B chooses an answer. Then switch.

1. **A:** Is this going to hurt?
   B: Yes, it's going to hurt a little.
   or: No, it isn't going to hurt.

2. **A:** Is this going to cost a lot?
   B: Yes, this is going to _____.
   or: No, this isn't going to _____.

3. **A:** Are you going to see a doctor soon?
   B: Yes, I'm _____.
   or: No, I'm _____.

4. **A:** Are your friends going to visit you?
   B: _____.

5. **A:** Is your insurance going to pay the doctor's bills?
   B: _____.

6. **A:** Are there going to be any risks with this test?
   B: _____.

Practice B

Imagine that your doctor has told you that you need an operation. Write three questions to ask about how the operation will affect you.

■■■■■ Read and Think

Read the materials below and circle the words you don't understand.
Then answer the questions that follow.

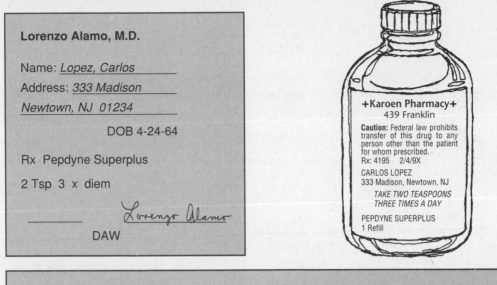

Lorenzo Alamo, M.D.

Name: *Lopez, Carlos*

Address: *333 Madison*

Newtown, NJ 01234

DOB 4-24-64

Rx Pepdyne Superplus

2 Tsp 3 x diem

_____ *Lorenzo Alamo*

DAW

+Karoen Pharmacy+
439 Franklin

Caution: Federal law prohibits transfer of this drug to any person other than the patient for whom prescribed.
Rx: 4195   2/4/9X
CARLOS LOPEZ
333 Madison, Newtown, NJ
TAKE TWO TEASPOONS THREE TIMES A DAY
PEPDYNE SUPERPLUS
1 Refill

Parkland Hospital
Your appointment is at _10 A.m._ on _Sept. 14_. Please arrive 15 minutes early.
First go to Outpatient Registration. They will direct you to the radiology department.

Do not eat anything after 8 P.M. the night before, and do not drink anything after midnight.

1. Where did Carlos take the prescription to be filled?
2. How much Pepdyne should Carlos take?
3. Carlos's brother has a stomachache. Should he take Pepdyne?
4. When should Carlos arrive at the hospital?
5. What time does Carlos have to go to the radiology department?
6. At what time can he eat his last meal before going to the hospital?

In Your Community

Find out the information individually or in groups and share it with
the class.

1. Find out from a doctor, nurse, pharmacist, or medical guide book what tests are used to diagnose the following ailments:

   ulcer   broken bone
   pneumonia   skin cancer
   AIDS   other: _____

2. Call the billing department at a local hospital and ask how much each of these tests costs. Make a chart with your classmates.

■ ■ ■ ■ ■ Figuring Out the U.S.

As you read the passage below, circle the words you don't understand and try to guess their meanings.

Alternative Health Care

"Healing is an art, not a science," many people say. There are no 100 percent guarantees with any treatment, and health professionals have different opinions about which treatments are best.

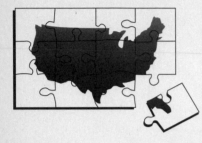

Most Americans choose M.D.s (medical doctors) as their health professionals. The medical approach to healing diseases includes the use of medicines, drugs, and surgery.

Other people choose different approaches to health care. Some people, for instance, go to a chiropractor when they have back pain. Chiropractors do not prescribe drugs or perform surgery. They help by moving the bones in the back and massaging the muscles.

People of certain religious beliefs (Christian Scientists, for example) do not go to doctors at all. They read the Bible and pray when they or someone in their family is ill. They depend on God and their inner spirits to heal the body.

Your Turn

Discuss the questions.

1. What does the phrase "Healing is an art, not a science" mean? Do you agree?
2. Have you ever recovered from a serious illness without treatment by a doctor or medication of any kind?
3. In your native country, where do you go when you are sick?
4. How is this different from going to a doctor or healer in the United States?
5. What choices for health care do you think are best for you and your family?

> *Choose one of the questions and write about it.*

6 Look at This Bill!

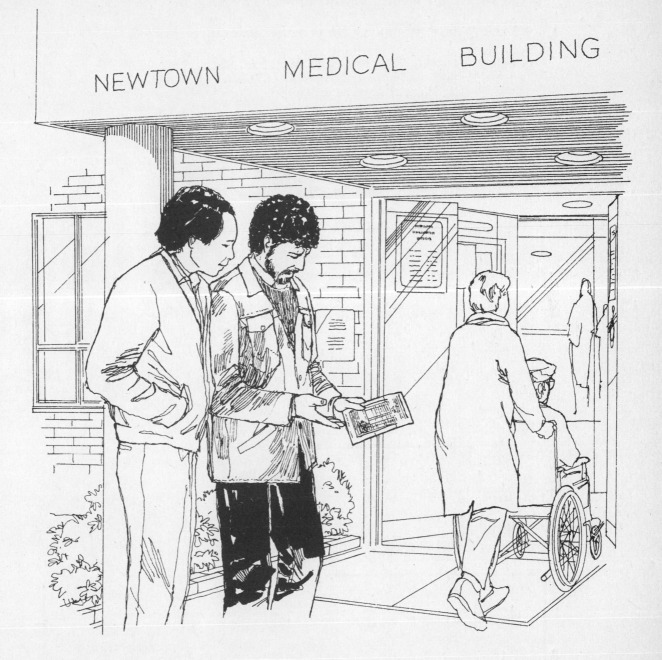

Before You Listen

1. Where are Carlos and Mike?
2. What do you think they are talking about?
3. How do you think Carlos feels?
4. What will Carlos do next?

■■■■■ Look at This Bill!

Listen carefully to the dialogue.

Carlos: I just went to the doctor. Look at this bill!

Mike: Seventy dollars! Do you have insurance?

Carlos: Through my job. But I'm not sure how it works.

_____

Carlos: Excuse me. Do you have a minute to explain something about our insurance policy?

Personnel manager: Sure. What do you need to know?

Carlos: I have a receipt from my doctor. How can I get reimbursed?

Personnel manager: Here. Fill in one of these claim forms. Make a copy of the receipt and attach the original to the claim form and send it in. They'll reimburse you for 80 percent of the bill. If you haven't met your deductible, you might have to pay the bill yourself.

Carlos: Does the policy cover blood tests?

Personnel manager: Yes, I think so. But let me check.

Words to Know		
bill	receipt	reimburse
insurance	claim form	deductible
_____	_____	_____

Another Way to Say It

They'll reimburse you.	They will repay you.
Here.	Here you are.
cover blood tests	pay for blood tests

■■■■■ Talking It Over

Discuss the questions in pairs or groups.

1. How much is the doctor's bill?
2. Does Carlos have health insurance?
3. What does Carlos have to do so the insurance company will reimburse him for his doctor's bills?
4. Why should Carlos make a copy of his receipt before he sends it?
5. Will the insurance company pay for blood tests?
6. Do you have health insurance? What does it cover?
7. Do you have insurance through your job, or do you pay for insurance yourself?

Working Together

Work with your classmates and teacher to finish the conversation below. Practice with a partner. Then write your own conversation.

Mike:	Could you tell me about our insurance coverage?
Personnel manager:	Certainly. What would you like to know?

Real Talk

The letter *c* in English may have a hard sound, like "k," or a soft sound, like "s." Listen as your teacher says the following words:

cover	claim	insurance	ulcer
cross	company	policy	medicine
doctor	copy	receipt	office

Look at the words. Can you think of a rule for telling when the letter *c* sounds like "k" and when it sounds like "s"?

■■■■■ Putting It Together

> **Future with _Will_**
>
> I/you/he/she/we/they **will** pay the bill today.
> I/you/he/she/we/they **will not** pay for any tests.
>
> In informal speech, use the contracted form: _I will = I'll_
> _I will not = I won't_

Work with a partner. Person A asks a question, and Person B chooses an answer. Then switch roles.

1. **A:** Will you go to the doctor soon?
   B: Yes, I'll go to the doctor soon.
   or: No, I won't go to the doctor soon.

2. **A:** Will your insurance company pay your medical bills?
   B: Yes, my insurance company will pay _____
   or: No, my insurance company won't pay _____

3. **A:** Will you make a copy of the bills for your records?
   B: _____

4. **A:** Will you file a claim for your medical bills?
   B: _____

5. **A:** Will your husband/wife/friend help you?
   B: _____

6. **A:** How much will the doctor charge?
   B: _____

7. **A:** Where will you buy the medicine?
   B: _____

8. **A:** When will you return to the doctor?
   B: _____

9. **A:** How often will you take the medicine?
   B: _____

10. **A:** _____
    B: _____

■■■■■ Read and Think

This is Carlos Lopez's medical insurance policy. As you read it, underline the words you don't know and discuss their meanings with the class. Then answer the questions below.

Guardian Benefit Mutual Group Health and Major Medical

Schedule of Coverage
Deductible amount $100
Coinsurance percentage   80%

Covered Charges

Hospital room and board	Ambulance service
Doctors' charges for surgery	Private-duty nursing
and other medical care	Drugs and medicine
X-ray exams and lab exams	Surgical dressings

Exclusions
Services or supplies not ordered by a doctor
Exams that are not needed for medical treatment
Charges to the extent that they exceed customary charges for this service
Examination and treatment of teeth
Eye examinations, eyeglasses
Sickness or injury due to war or while in military service

---

1. Will this insurance policy cover surgery? drugs and medicine? X-ray exams? checkup exams? dentist's bills? eyeglasses?
2. What is a *deductible*? How much is the deductible on this policy?
3. What does *coinsurance percentage* mean? How much is the coinsurance percentage on this policy?
4. Carlos went to the doctor. He also had X-rays and a blood test. The total of the fees is $400. How much of that cost will the insurance company pay?

In Your Community

Find out the information individually or in groups and share it with the class.

1. Find out the charges for the following services at two different doctors' offices or clinics: An office visit   An annual checkup
          A flu shot   A chest X-ray
2. Call a local hospital to find out the cost of a day in the hospital in a semiprivate room, a private room, and in intensive care.
3. Call a health insurance company to find out the cost of individual and group health insurance. Compare the costs.

■■■■■■ Figuring Out the U.S.

As you read the passage below, circle the words you don't understand and try to guess their meanings.

Health Insurance

The United States does not have a national health insurance plan for all of its citizens. Instead, many Americans have insurance through their jobs. They pay lower rates because they pay as part of a group.

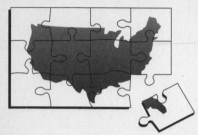

Other Americans work for companies that don't have insurance plans, or they work for themselves. These people have difficult choices to make. Insurance coverage for a working family can cost more than $300 a month. But if one member of the family gets very sick, medical care may cost thousands of dollars.

Here is a sample insurance policy application form. Fill it out as if it were yours.

Guardian Benefit Mutual
Application for Hospital, Surgical, and Medical Expenses Policy

Name _____

Address _____

Home Telephone _____ Work Telephone _____

Occupation _____

Names of persons to be insured	Date of birth			Age	Sex	Relationship to applicant	Marital status
	Mo.	Day	Yr.		M F		

Premiums payable Annually [ ] Semiannually [ ] Quarterly [ ] Monthly [ ]

Signature   Date

_____   _____

Your Turn

Discuss the questions.

1. What are two ways of getting health insurance in the U.S.?
2. In your native country, who pays for health care? individuals? employers? the government?
3. Do you think that system works well?
4. Individual health insurance is very expensive. Do you think it is better to pay the cost or save the money and hope to stay healthy?

> *Choose one of the questions and write about it.*

Person A

Work with a partner. Look at this page only, and your partner will look at page 40 only.

   Each of you will look at a picture of a doctor's office. Your pictures are similar, but they are not exactly alike. There are eight differences between the two pictures. Find out what the differences are by asking questions. **Do not look at your partner's picture.**

Person B

Work with a partner. Look at this page only, and your partner will look at page 39 only.

Each of you will look at a picture of a doctor's office. Your pictures are similar, but they are not exactly alike. There are eight differences between the two pictures. Find out what the differences are by asking questions. **Do not look at your partner's picture.**

Before You Listen

1. What office is this?
2. One patient is standing by the reception desk. What do you think she is asking the clerk?
3. What are the other people doing?
4. How will they know when it's their turn to talk to the caseworker?
5. How long do you think they will have to wait?

■ ■ ■ ■ ■ We Can't Pay the Doctor's Bills

Listen carefully to the dialogue.

Olga: I'd like to apply for Medicare, please.

Clerk: Medicare is only for people over 65 or disabled people on Social Security.

Olga: Oh. Then I mean Medicaid.

Clerk: All right. You have to make an appointment and show that you are eligible.

Olga: How do I know if I'm eligible?

Clerk: Are you a resident of this county?

Olga: Yes.

Clerk: Do you have children?

Olga: Yes—one daughter, and I'm expecting a baby.

Clerk: Do you have a job?

Olga: Yes. I work as a waitress. But my husband is unemployed. We can't pay the doctor's bills.

Clerk: What are your earnings?

Olga: I earn $250 a week, but I'm seven months pregnant, and I have to stop working soon.

Words to Know

disabled	resident	unemployed
eligible	county	earnings
_____	_____	_____

Another Way to Say It

can't afford .... don't have enough money for

_____ .... _____

■■■■■ Talking It Over

Discuss the questions in pairs or groups.

1. What does Olga want?
2. What does she need to do?
3. Does Olga have children?
4. What is Olga's job? How much does she earn at her job?
5. Does Olga's husband have a job?
6. Why will Olga stop working soon?
7. Can she afford the doctor's bills?
8. What will she do if she's not eligible for Medicaid?
9. In your native country, do people need to prove that they are eligible for government health programs?
10. In your native country, do pregnant women work?

Working Together

Work with a partner. Person A will be a clerk in a public aid office. Person B will call to get information about Medicaid. Person B should ask questions like these:

How old do you have to be to qualify?
Do you have to be a citizen?
Are permanent residents eligible?
What papers or documents do I need?

Person A should answer. Make up the answers if you don't know them.

Real Talk

The letter *g* has two different sounds. Listen to your teacher say the following words:

get	government	pregnant
eligible	dosage	radiologist

Gerunds and Infinitives

Olga enjoys   **working**   at the restaurant.
She plans   **to work**   until the baby comes.

Gerunds	**Infinitives**
The *-ing* form is used	The *to* form is used after
after these verbs:	these verbs:
enjoy (working)	plan (to work)
can't stop	need
avoid	expect
keep on	promise
	refuse
	afford

To know which form to use, memorize these lists and add to them.

Practice A

Complete each sentence. Use the correct form of a word from the list below. The first one is done for you.

quit   ~~work~~   look   have
ask   think   pay   sleep

1. Olga enjoys __working__ at the restaurant.

2. She expects _____ in two months, when the baby comes.

3. She wants _____ the baby at the hospital.

4. She can't afford _____ the doctor's bills.

5. She can't stop _____ about her money problems.

6. She refuses _____ her parents for help.

Practice B

Work with a partner. Ask each other questions about things you need to do and things you enjoy doing.

Example: *Do you need to go to the dentist?*
        Do you enjoy going to the dentist?

■■■■■ Read and Think

Read the passage and try to guess the meanings of the underlined words. Rephrase each paragraph. Then answer the questions that follow.

Medicaid and Medicare

In the United States, the government pays for some people's health care costs. Medicaid and Medicare are two government health programs.

Medicaid is a national program that pays for the health care of very poor people. Each state has different Medicaid <u>regulations</u>. In the state of New Jersey, for example, only these people are eligible: pregnant women, children under 2, people 65 and over, blind people, and <u>disabled</u> people who receive monthly Supplemental Security Income (SSI) payments. However, not all doctors will accept Medicaid as payment. To find out more about Medicaid, call your state's Department of Public Aid.

Medicare is a health insurance program for people older than 65 and certain disabled people. It has two parts: Medicare A and Medicare B. Medicare A covers the cost of <u>hospitalization</u> and doctors' services in the hospital. Medicare B covers doctors' services outside the hospital. If you are <u>collecting</u> Social Security, the government will pay for Medicare A. If you are not collecting Social Security but are over 65 and have lived in the U.S. for five years, you may be able to purchase Medicare coverage. You can apply for Medicare through the Social Security Administration.

1. Who is eligible for Medicaid? Where can you apply for it?
2. Will all doctors accept Medicaid?
3. In general, who is eligible for Medicare? Where can you apply for it?

In Your Community

Work in pairs or groups to find out the following information. Report to the class.

1. What government office handles Medicaid in your area? Call or visit that office and ask how someone can apply. Find out who qualifies for Medicaid.
2. Ask a number of doctors, dentists, and chiropractors if they accept Medicaid patients. Ask those who do not accept Medicaid patients to explain why.
3. Talk about Medicare with a retired person receiving Social Security payments. Ask how much Medicare costs and what it covers.

▪▪▪▪▪ Figuring Out the U.S.

As you read the passage, circle the words you don't understand and try to guess their meanings.

Red Tape

When you deal with a government agency, there are usually many procedures to follow, and many delays. These long procedures and delays are called **red tape**. Red tape often seems intended to drive people crazy.

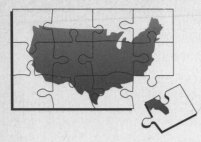

Imagine that you want to apply for Medicaid or food stamps. First, you check the telephone book to find the number of the agency you want. The line probably will be busy for a long time. Then, the person who finally answers your call may tell you to call a different department. And when you call that number, you may get a recording or get put on hold. When you finally make an appointment, you may have to wait a long time—weeks or months—to see someone. You will have to produce many documents to prove your age, residence, income, and eligibility.

On the day of your appointment, you may sit in a waiting room for hours. Your case may be unusual, and the caseworker may have to transfer you to a supervisor or send you to a different department. In some cases, the computer breaks down or your records get lost, and you have to start all over again.

It takes patience and persistence to apply for AFDC (Aid to Families with Dependent Children), food stamps, or Medicaid.

Your Turn

Discuss the questions.

1. What is "red tape"? Give three examples.
2. Have you ever called or visited a government agency in the U.S.?
3. Is "red tape" common in your native country?
4. Does your telephone book have a section for government agencies' numbers? Are you familiar with some of the agencies? Which ones?
5. What advice about paying for health care would you give to a person who has just arrived in the U.S.?

> *Choose one of the questions and write about it.*

This Is an Emergency!

Before You Listen

1. What do you think has happened?
2. What is Olga putting on Pavel? Why?
3. What time of year is it? How can you tell?
4. What do you think will happen next?

■ ■ ■ ■ ■ **This Is an Emergency!**

Listen carefully to the dialogue.

Dispatcher: Ambulance service.

Mike: This is an emergency! Please send an ambulance right away.

Dispatcher: What's the address?

Mike: 44 Center Street.

Dispatcher: Can you tell me what happened?

Mike: My neighbor, Pavel Vrana, fell on the ice. He's badly hurt. He hit his head. I think he broke his leg, too.

Dispatcher: Is he able to move?

Mike: No. He's unconscious.

Dispatcher: Keep him covered, but don't move him in case there is an injury to his neck or spine.

Mike: Right.

Dispatcher: We'll have an ambulance there in five minutes. Are you a relative?

Mike: No—a neighbor.

Dispatcher: Can you ride with him to the hospital to give information?

Mike: Of course. I'll call his daughter, too, and tell her what happened.

Words to Know

emergency	injury	relative
ambulance	spine	neighbor
unconscious		
_____	_____	_____

Another Way to Say It

to provide information .... to answer questions
Are you a relative? .... Are you a member of his family?
Right. .... OK.

_____ .... _____

▪▪▪▪▪ Talking It Over

Discuss the questions in pairs or groups.

1. Who does Mike talk to? What number do you think he dialed?
2. What other numbers can you call in an emergency?
3. What happened to Pavel?
4. What advice did the dispatcher give Mike?
5. How long will it take the ambulance to get there? Is that a long time?
6. How does Mike know Pavel?
7. Have you ever ridden in an ambulance? For what reason?
8. What other emergencies require an ambulance?

Working Together

Look at the picture. There was a bad accident, and many people were hurt.
Work with a partner to finish the conversation below. Person A describes
the scene to Person B, an ambulance dispatcher. Use words like *lying*,
burning, and *crying*. Person B asks questions. Then switch roles.

Person A: This is an emergency! We need an ambulance.
Person B: Can you tell me what's happening now?

Real Talk

The short "a" sound in English does not exist in some other languages.
Listen as your teacher says the following words:

ambulance	address	can
happened	man	that

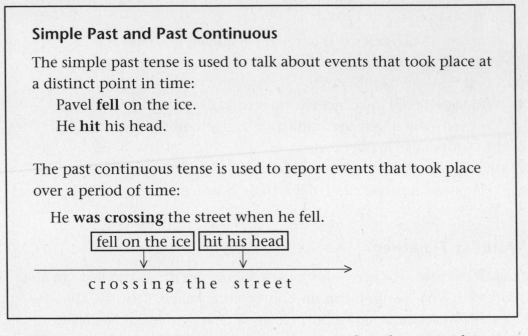

Simple Past and Past Continuous

The simple past tense is used to talk about events that took place at a distinct point in time:

Pavel **fell** on the ice.

He **hit** his head.

The past continuous tense is used to report events that took place over a period of time:

He **was crossing** the street when he fell.

In the emergency room, patients must sometimes describe an accident to a nurse, doctor, or police officer. Below is a conversation between Pavel and a nurse.

Read the dialogue and fill in the blanks with the correct verb in the past continuous tense. Follow the example.

Nurse: What were you doing when the accident happened?

Pavel: I ___was walking___ across the street. I looked up.
(*walk*)

I saw that a car _____ into the intersection.
(*turn*)

The driver _____ the other way. I tried to run, but
(*look*)

I slipped and fell on the ice. I hit my head and was knocked out.

Nurse: When you regained consciousness, what _____ ?
(*happen*)

Pavel: My friend Mike _____ me, "Are you OK?"
(*ask*)

My leg _____ . I heard sirens in the distance.
(*bleed*)

I think the ambulance _____ .
(*arrive*)

■■■■■ Read and Think

Read the passage and try to guess the meanings of the underlined words. Rephrase each paragraph. Then answer the questions.

At the Emergency Room

Doctors are not usually available at night or on weekends. People who are seriously ill or injured may go to the emergency room at those times.

The emergency room of a hospital is open 24 hours a day. When there are many emergencies, the doctors treat the most <u>serious</u> cases, such as stopped breathing, heart attacks, and <u>severe</u> bleeding, first. A person with a broken leg may be in a lot of pain, but a broken leg is not <u>life threatening</u>, and so that person may have to wait.

You have to fill out an <u>intake form</u> when you use the emergency room. When you sign the form, you are giving <u>permission</u> for the treatment and promising to pay the bill. The form also asks your <u>religion</u> and the name of your <u>next of kin</u>, a close family member.

Most hospitals have a list of the different languages that their doctors, nurses, <u>aides</u>, and other employees speak. When a person who comes to the emergency room cannot speak English, it is sometimes possible to find someone who speaks the same language to <u>interpret</u>. You may want to keep a copy of your health history in English in your wallet also.

1. What are three life-threatening conditions that will be treated first in an emergency room?
2. What information is requested on the emergency room intake form?
3. What help may there be if you don't speak English very well and you have to go to the emergency room of a hospital?
4. How can you be prepared for an emergency room visit?

In Your Community

Find out the information individually or in groups and share it with the class.

1. What number can people call for emergency service?
2. What hospital does your local ambulance usually take patients to?
3. Are there courses in first aid given at your school or in your community? If so, find out the location, time, and costs of the courses.

■ ■ ■ ■ ■ ■ Figuring Out the U.S.

As you read the passage below, circle the words you don't understand and try to guess their meanings.

For Emergencies Only?

Some people go to emergency rooms for minor medical problems. They may not have a regular doctor, and they use the emergency room of their local hospital for all of their medical needs.

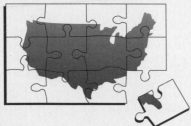

Emergency rooms have all the necessary equipment for tests and other treatments. There is always a doctor on duty, 24 hours a day, and many people cannot see a doctor during regular office hours. Also, some insurance plans make it easier to get reimbursed if medical care is given in a hospital rather than in a doctor's office.

But there can be problems with using the emergency room in a nonemergency. When you are ill, it is better to have a doctor or health-care professional who knows you. That person takes your entire medical history into consideration. An emergency room doctor usually sees a patient just once, and there may not be any follow-up care. Also, the patient may have to wait a long time, and the doctor may be very rushed.

Many communities now have medical offices that are open 18 to 24 hours a day. These offices take a lot of pressure off those who work in hospital emergency rooms.

Your Turn

Discuss the questions.

1. Where can you go if you or a member of your family has a medical problem at night?
2. Have you ever gone to an emergency room? What was it like?
3. Are you calm during emergencies?
4. In your native country, what do people do in a medical emergency?
5. How would you like medical care in the U.S. to be different from the way it is now?

> **Choose one of the questions and write about it.**

9 | Which Tooth Is Bothering You?

Before You Listen

1. Where is Mike?
2. What is the dentist doing?
3. Who is standing next to the dental chair?
4. What machines can you see?
5. What is on the wall?
6. How often do you go to a dentist? Why do you go?

■■■■■ Which Tooth Is Bothering You?

Listen carefully to the dialogue.

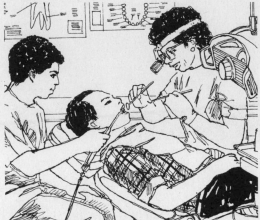

Dr. Ford: Which tooth is bothering you?

Mike: The big tooth on the upper left.

Dr. Ford: Mm-hmm. You have a big cavity.

Mike: Will you have to pull the tooth?

Dr. Ford: No, I think we can save it. I'll schedule you for a root canal.

Mike: What's a root canal?

Dr. Ford: The cavity in your tooth has reached the nerve. When we do a root canal, we drill down into each root of the tooth. We remove the nerves and then fill the tooth.

Mike: I should have come sooner.

Dr. Ford: Yes, people should have their teeth checked twice a year. Filling a small cavity is easier than filling a large one.

Mike: Does a root canal hurt much?

Dr. Ford: No. I'll give you an anesthetic to numb that area. You won't feel a thing.

Mike: I don't have insurance. Which would cost more—having the tooth pulled or having the root canal?

Dr. Ford: The root canal is more expensive at first. Losing a tooth is more expensive in the long run.

Words to Know

cavity	nerve	fill
root canal	drill	anesthetic
_____	_____	_____

Another Way to Say It

pull a tooth .... extract a tooth

in the long run .... ultimately

_____ .... _____

■■■■■ Talking It Over

Discuss the questions in pairs or groups.

1. What is Mike's problem?
2. Which tooth is bothering him?
3. Does he have a small cavity or a large one?
4. Will the dentist have to pull the tooth?
5. How can the dentist save it?
6. Why is Mike worried about the root canal?
7. How often should people go to the dentist?
8. What do dentists give to avoid pain when they fill cavities?
9. Did you go to a dentist this year?
10. Did you have any cavities?
11. Did the dentist fill them?
12. Did the dentist give you an anesthetic?

Working Together

Imagine you have a very bad toothache and the dentist is asking you to choose between having the tooth pulled out and having a root canal. Work with your classmates and teacher to finish the conversation below. Then practice with a partner.

Patient: Will it hurt to have the tooth pulled?
Dentist: No. I'll give you an anesthetic.

Real Talk

The "v" sound and the "b" sound are distinct in English. Listen as your teacher says the following words. Pronounce them carefully, placing your upper teeth against your lower lip to make the "v" sound and bringing both lips together to make the "b" sound.

cavity	silver	bothering
save	every	big
nerve		

> ## Modals: Should/Shouldn't
>
> You **should** see a dentist about your toothache.
> You **shouldn't** wait too long.
>
> Use *should* or *shouldn't* to give advice.
> Reminder: *Should* is always followed by the simple form of a verb.

Work with a partner. Person A asks a question. Person B gives advice,
using *should*.

1. **A:** What should I do to keep my teeth healthy?
   B: You should brush your teeth after every meal.

2. **A:** How often should children go for checkups?
   B: _____

3. **A:** My brother has a toothache. What should he do?
   B: _____

4. **A:** How should I remove food that's stuck between my teeth?
   B: _____

5. **A:** What should I eat to keep my teeth healthy?
   B: _____

■■■■■ Read and Think

Read the passage and try to guess the meanings of the underlined words.
Rephrase each paragraph. Then answer the questions.

Caring for Your Teeth

Teeth do a lot of work chewing three meals or more a day. They also affect a person's appearance and speech. If a tooth is missing, other teeth will start to <u>loosen</u>. With teeth missing, a person can't chew properly, and the <u>jawbone</u> starts to <u>weaken</u>. Other teeth will soon fall out.

Caring for teeth is not difficult, but it does require a daily routine. To take better care of your teeth, you should brush your teeth after every meal and <u>floss</u> between your teeth once a day. Have your teeth cleaned twice a year to stop <u>plaque</u> from building up on them, and have any cavities filled. Some dentists paint children's teeth with <u>fluoride</u> or recommend a fluoride rinse to strengthen the <u>enamel</u> of the teeth. Some children get <u>braces</u> to straighten teeth, to improve appearance and correct poor chewing. However, braces are very expensive.

Twenty years ago, one-third of older Americans wore <u>dentures</u>, or false teeth. Today, there are many more older people, but more than 80 percent of them still have their original teeth. This is partly because more people are getting dental care.

1. What happens when a tooth is missing?
2. What are three ways of taking care of teeth?
3. What is the purpose of a fluoride mouthwash?
4. What can a dentist do to help care for teeth?
5. Why are more Americans keeping their teeth?

In Your Community

Find out the information individually or in groups and share it with the class.

1. Find out the cost of the following dental work: one-surface filling, a three-surface filling, an extraction, a root-canal job, a crown for one tooth, a bridge for four teeth, a complete set of dentures.
2. Talk to someone whose child wears braces. Ask whether the braces cause any discomfort, how long they must be worn, and how much they cost.

■ ■ ■ ■ ■ Figuring Out the U.S.

As you read the passage below, circle the words you don't understand and try to guess their meanings.

Painless Visits to the Dentist

Many people are afraid to go to the dentist, but dentists are trying hard to change that. Some dentists specialize in "painless" dentistry. They want to make the patient's visit a pleasant one.

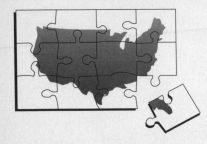

Dentists use drills when they fill a cavity. But their drills work quietly and at very high speeds. Anesthetics, or painkillers, numb the nerves so there is little or no pain. The dentist can even apply medication so the patient doesn't feel the needle for the anesthetic.

In some offices, windows offer views of parks or bird feeders, and patients can listen to music through headphones while the dentist works. There may be toys and stuffed animals for children to play with.

Your Turn

Discuss the questions.

1. Do you think "painless" dentistry is a good idea?
2. In your native country, where did you go when you had a toothache or needed to get your teeth cleaned? How was it different from going to the dentist in the U.S.?
3. Do you get nervous when you go to the dentist? What are some ways to relax before going?
4. Do you prefer to get an anesthetic when you have a cavity filled?
5. What are some side effects from anesthetic?
6. Do you think it is important to avoid having your teeth pulled?

> *Choose one of the questions and write about it.*

Person A

Work with a partner. Look at this page only, and your partner will look at page 60 only. Take turns asking each other for definitions of the words missing from the puzzle.

Example: **Person A:**   *What's number one down?*
                Person B: *It's frozen water. It's very cold.*

Do not use the exact word or a form of the word in your definition. Write in the words going **down**. The first answer is written for you.

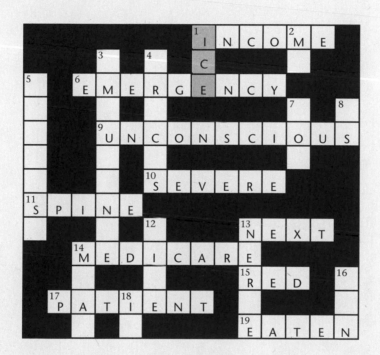

Person B

Work with a partner. Look at this page only, and your partner will look at page 59. Take turns asking each other for definitions of the words missing from the puzzle.

Example: ***Person B:*** *What's number one across?*

Person A: *It's money you get when you work. You have to pay this kind of tax every year.*

Do not use the exact word or a form of the word in your definition. Write in the words going **across**. The first answer is written for you.

Do You Worry Much?

Before You Listen

1. Where is Carlos?
2. Who is the woman with him?
3. Why do you think Carlos has come here?
4. In your native country, do people talk about their problems and worries?
5. Where do people go to get advice?

■■■■■ Do You Worry Much?

Listen carefully to the dialogue.

Ms. Wendon: Hello, Mr. Lopez. I'm Ms. Wendon. Dr. Alamo asked me to speak with you.

Carlos: Do I have anything serious?

Ms. Wendon: Oh, no. But Dr. Alamo thinks that your stomach pains may be caused by stress, or anxiety.

Carlos: What do you mean?

Ms. Wendon: Sometimes worries and problems can affect your body and make you ill. Do you worry much?

Carlos: Well, yes. I do. Frequently I can't sleep, or I have nightmares.

Ms. Wendon: What happens in your nightmares?

Carlos: Sometimes I dream that I'll never speak English well enough to make more money. I worry about my wife, Luz, and our little girl. I often worry about my parents back in the Dominican Republic.

Ms. Wendon: It's very hard moving to a new country, isn't it? Moving away from family and friends, leaving behind everything that is familiar to you. . . .

Carlos: Yes, it is. I feel as though I have no control over my life.

Words to Know

stress	worries	familiar
anxiety	nightmares	control
_____	_____	_____

Another Way to Say It

I can't sleep. .... I have insomnia.
get rid of .... stop, end
_____ .... _____

■■■■■ Talking It Over

Discuss the questions in pairs or groups.

1. Can anxieties affect your body and cause illness?
2. Is life in the U.S. hard or easy for Carlos?
3. Does Carlos sleep well at night?
4. What is a nightmare?
5. What does Carlos worry about?
6. Do you worry about the same things?
7. Is Ms. Wendon a medical doctor? What is her job?
8. Do you think people go to counselors or therapists in Carlos's native country?
9. Do people go to counselors or therapists in your native country? If not, who do they talk to about their problems?
10. What do you think a therapist can do for someone who is worried?

Working Together

Work with a partner. Person A: Imagine you are Carlos's wife, father, or mother. Tell what you worry about. Use words like *always*, *often*, and *sometimes*. Person B: Imagine you are a counselor. Listen to Person A and ask questions. Then switch.

Person A: I worry about my son Carlos. He doesn't have enough money for his family.

Person B: Do you think about this often?

Real Talk

Some English words that come from the Greek language begin with a silent *p*. Listen as your teacher says the following words:

psychologist   **p**sychosomatic   **pn**eumonia
psychotherapy   **p**sychosis   **ps**oriasis
psychiatrist

■■■■■ Putting It Together

Frequency Words

	Percentage of the time
always	100%
usually	80–99%
often	50–80%
frequently	50–80%
sometimes	5–60%
occasionally	5–20%
seldom	1–5%
never	0%

Frequency words can be placed after the verb *be*, before the main verb, and sometimes at the beginning or end of the sentence.

Sam is **usually** late.

Chung **always** comes on time.

Sometimes Sam is on time.

Sam is on time **sometimes**.

Practice A

Complete each sentence correctly according to the dialogue on page 62. Use frequency words from the list above.

1. Carlos _____ worries about his parents.
2. His stomach _____ hurts.
3. He _____ can sleep at night.
4. He has nightmares _____.
5. _____ he dreams about not being able to speak English.

Practice B

Answer the following questions using frequency words.

1. How often are you absent from class?
2. How often do you get a cold?
3. Can you understand people when they speak English quickly?
4. Do you worry about your family?
5. Are you ever sick?

■■■■■ Read and Think

Read the passage and try to guess the meanings of the underlined words. Rephrase each paragraph. Then answer the questions.

Mental Health Resources

In <u>stressful</u> situations, people sometimes need to turn to others in order to stay mentally healthy. They feel better when they can discuss their deep feelings with an understanding person. Sometimes friends and family are the best source of support in times of difficulty. A <u>minister</u>, <u>priest</u>, or <u>rabbi</u> may be able to help, too.

Many kinds of specialists help people learn to <u>cope</u> with their problems. For instance, <u>marriage</u> <u>counselors</u> work with couples who are fighting or can't communicate. <u>Family</u> <u>counselors</u> see an entire family. <u>Social</u> <u>workers</u> may work with just one person or with a group.

There are also <u>self-help</u> groups for people who are coping with such problems as <u>divorce</u>, <u>disability</u>, <u>drug</u> <u>addiction</u>, or <u>alcoholism</u>. Many of these groups are free of charge.

If you have a problem but don't want to see anyone face-to-face, you can call a telephone <u>hot</u> <u>line</u>. Callers usually don't have to give their names or any other information about themselves. When a person talks to a hot-line worker, counselor, or other specialist, all information is kept <u>confidential</u>, or secret. The specialist should not tell anyone else what the person said.

1. What is stress? What kinds of problems can cause stress?
2. Name two ways family and friends can help us cope with stress.
3. Name some specialists in mental health. How are they different?
4. What do you think a self-help group is?

In Your Community

Find out the information individually or in groups and share it with the class.

1. Look in the front of the phone book for a list of "community services" numbers. What organizations are listed? Call several of them and ask what services they offer.
2. Check the yellow pages of the phone book under "Counseling," "Psychologists," and "Mental Health Services." Are there professionals who speak your native language? How would you find out? How would you find out if these professionals are competent and well trained?

■■■■■ Figuring Out the U.S.

As you read the passage below, circle the words you don't understand and try to guess their meanings.

Asking for Help

Fifty years ago, most Americans would not consider going to a psychotherapist, or counselor. They thought that "strong" people handled problems alone. But today it is becoming more common to see a therapist for anxiety, phobias (fears), depression, and other emotional problems.

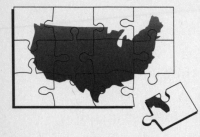

Many people go to therapists to seek help with both temporary and long-term problems. They may go to a therapist or counselor in private practice or to a mental health clinic where fees are on a sliding scale—that is, they are adjusted according to each client's income.

Some people prefer to "shop around" to find a therapist they like. For instance, it may be important for the counselor to speak the person's native language very well.

In addition to individual therapy and counseling, there are short-term classes, groups, or retreats where individuals or couples can receive help managing their lives or their relationships. The local clinic may have information on most of these.

Your Turn

Discuss the questions.

1. In your native country, is drug addiction a problem? alcoholism? unemployment? divorce?
2. In your native country, how do people cope with emotional problems?
3. Do you think that "strong people" handle problems alone?
4. Imagine that you need to talk about a problem. Would you rather talk to someone who speaks your native language? someone who is from your native country? someone who is your age? a man? a woman?

> *Choose one of the questions and write about it.*

11 | That's Why It's Called Labor

Before You Listen

1. Where do you think Olga and Mike are?
2. What are they preparing for?
3. What do you think Mike will do during the baby's birth?
4. In your native country, how do women prepare for childbirth? Do they go to classes?
5. Do men help women prepare for childbirth? How?
6. What do you think prenatal checkups are?

■■■■■ That's Why It's Called Labor

Listen carefully to the dialogue.

Nurse: That's the end of our class for tonight. Any questions?

Olga: Yes. I heard that it's not safe to take over-the-counter medicines like aspirin. Is that true?

Nurse: Check with your obstetrician. Some medicines do affect the baby's development. It's good to avoid drugs, alcohol, caffeine, and cigarettes, too.

Mike: Is having a baby very painful?

Nurse: The pain comes from fear. When a woman understands what happens during labor, she will be less afraid. It's a hard job she has to do. That's why it's called "labor."

Olga: Can I get painkillers?

Nurse: Yes. You can ask for anesthesia so you won't feel the pain. But the baby gets the anesthesia too. It's healthier for the baby if you can do without painkillers.

Mike: Can I be with my wife in the delivery room?

Nurse: Yes, if you both want that. You can help with her breathing during the contractions. You'll be her coach.

Words to Know

obstetrician	caffeine	delivery room
development	labor	coach
avoid	anesthesia	
_____	_____	_____

Another Way to Say It

do without painkillers .... not use painkillers

contractions .... labor pains

_____ .... _____

■■■■■ Talking It Over

Discuss the questions in pairs or groups.

1. Where are Mike and Olga?
2. Do you think Olga has given birth before? Why or why not?
3. What things should a pregnant woman avoid?
4. What kind of doctor delivers babies?
5. Does the nurse say that childbirth is painful? Do you agree?
6. Can Olga get painkillers during the baby's birth?
7. What happens to the baby if the mother gets anesthesia?
8. Can Mike be with Olga during the baby's birth?
9. Do you think fathers should be allowed in delivery rooms?
10. What can a father do to prepare for the birth of a child?

Working Together

Work with a partner. Person A: Imagine that you are a pregnant woman. You want your husband to be in the delivery room when your baby is born. (If you are a man, imagine you are the woman's husband.)
Person B: Imagine that you are a traditional doctor. You give reasons why the husband should not be allowed in the delivery room. Person A's job is to try to change the doctor's mind. Then switch roles.

Real Talk

In English, *th* has two different sounds. Watch your teacher's teeth and tongue as he or she says *breathe* and *breath*. Look in a mirror when you practice.

Now practice the following words with your teacher:

bir**th**	bir**th**ing
anes**th**esia	bo**th**er
mon**th**	brea**th**ing
heal**th**y	**th**ey

Example: *Many women have a heal**th**y bir**th** without anes**th**esia.*

Comparisons

To make a comparison,
add *-er* to the adjective:
Dr. Shapiro is **taller** than Olga.
If the word ends in *-y*, drop
the *-y* and replace it with an *-i*:
easy + *-er* = easier
For longer words, put *more* before
the adjective:
A Caesarian delivery is
more expensive than a regular
delivery.

Practice A

Look at the picture in the box. Fill in the blanks below with the comparative forms of these adjectives: *tall, short, long, old,* and *young*.

1. Olga is not very tall. She is _____ than Dr. Shapiro.

2. Dr. Shapiro is 61 years old. She is _____ than Olga.

3. Olga's hair is _____ than Dr. Shapiro's hair.

Practice B

Work with a partner. Person A asks a question and Person B answers it. Then switch roles. The first one is done as an example.

1. A: Which is more important for a pregnant woman, good nutrition or good clothing?
   B: Good nutrition is more important than good clothing.

2. A: Which is worse for a pregnant woman, alcohol or soda?
   B: _____

3. A: Which is more painful, going to the dentist or having a baby?
   B: _____

4. A: Which is more difficult, having a baby or paying for the delivery?
   B: _____

■■■■■ Read and Think

Read the passage and try to guess the meanings of the underlined words. Rephrase each paragraph. Then answer the questions.

Tests during Pregnancy

Many doctors test pregnant women to find out if their babies will be born healthy. If a woman's test results are not normal, the doctor will <u>monitor</u> the baby's development more carefully.

For instance, doctors perform blood tests for diseases such as <u>syphilis</u> and AIDS. If a woman is sick, her baby will probably be born with the same illness. Doctors also test for the <u>Rh factor</u>, a substance in the blood. There can be problems if a woman's Rh factor is negative and her husband's Rh factor is positive.

Doctors use <u>ultrasound</u> to view the baby to be sure it is developing normally. The ultrasound tests can also show if the baby is a boy or a girl. Some doctors avoid using ultrasound because they are not sure it is 100 percent safe.

If there is a high risk of a <u>birth defect</u>, a doctor may perform a test called <u>amniocentesis</u>. The doctor inserts a needle through the woman's abdomen and takes a sample of the <u>amniotic</u> fluid to test. This test has risks too, so it is not advised for young, healthy mothers.

1. Why do doctors perform tests during pregnancy?
2. Why does a doctor test a pregnant woman's blood?
3. Do all doctors believe ultrasound is 100 percent safe? Do you think the other tests are 100 percent safe?
4. What is the purpose of an amniocentesis?
5. What else can women do so that their babies are born healthy?

In Your Community

Find out the information individually or in groups and share it with the class.

1. Ask several mothers what kinds of tests their doctors did during their pregnancies.
2. Call the local hospital(s) to find out about their facilities for delivering babies. Are fathers allowed in the delivery rooms? Are babies kept in the mother's hospital room or in a nursery?

■■■■■ Figuring Out the U.S.

As you read the passage, circle the words you do not understand and try to guess their meanings.

Birthing Options

In the U.S., most babies are born in hospitals. Traditionally, the mother gives birth in a hospital delivery room, and the father waits outside.

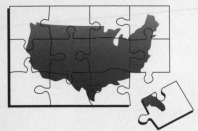

Some women feel that the hospital rooms are too sterile and not homey. But they want to give birth in a hospital in case there are complications. As a result, some hospitals now provide special "birthing rooms." These rooms are decorated like bedrooms, and a woman can have family members with her during the birth.

Instead of lying down, the woman can sit in a special birthing chair. Sitting up is a more natural position for giving birth.

The father may assist during the birth. The nurses show him how to cut the umbilical cord that connects the baby to the mother. Then the baby is washed and placed in the mother's arms. The room is warm and the lights are dim so that the baby will not be shocked by cold air or bright lights.

Many families want to have babies at home, using natural childbirth methods. A midwife is specially trained to assist births at home. Home birth is cheaper, and the parents plan to go to the hospital right away if there is a problem. However, midwifery is illegal in some states.

Your Turn

Discuss the questions.

1. In your native country, where are babies born?
2. Who delivers babies?
3. Who else is present when babies are born?
4. In your native country, have childbirth methods changed in the last 10 or 20 years?
5. Where do you think it is best to have a baby—in a hospital, at home, or somewhere else?
6. Who do you think should be present at a birth? Why?

> *Choose one of the questions and write about it.*

12 | What's for Supper?

Before You Listen

1. Where are Mike and Olga?
2. What is Mike doing?
3. What do you think they will eat for supper?
4. Who will cook the meal—Mike or Olga?
5. Is it hard to work and find time to cook a good meal? Why or why not?

■■■■■ What's for Supper?

Listen carefully to the dialogue.

Mike: What's for supper?

Olga: Pizza. I'll heat it up right now.

Mike: I thought the doctor recommended fresh vegetables.

Olga: She did, but I don't feel like cooking. Frozen food is easier.

Mike: And didn't she say to avoid coffee?

Olga: This is my only cup today.

Mike: What about milk? Did you drink any milk today?

Olga: Well . . . not much. But I did take my vitamins.

Mike: Vitamins without good food can't do much good. What did you have for lunch?

Olga: I didn't have much time for lunch. I had a bowl of soup.

Mike: That's it?

Olga: Mike, I know you want the best of everything for our baby. I do, too. But I'm so tired.

Mike: I'm sorry. Of course you are. What can I do to help?

Olga: Could you do the shopping? We need a lot of things: brown rice, whole wheat bread, carrots, oranges, skim milk, fish, tofu . . .

Mike: Wait. I can't remember all that!

Olga: You're right. I'll make a list.

Words to Know

supper	frozen	tofu
vegetables	vitamins	list
_____	_____	_____

Another Way to Say It

I don't feel like cooking. .... I'm not in the mood to cook.

can't do much good............................ aren't very helpful

_____ .... _____

■■■■■ Talking It Over

Discuss the questions in pairs or groups.

1. What is Olga making for supper?
2. What did the doctor recommend?
3. Why can't Mike and Olga eat a better meal tonight?
4. How do you think Mike feels? How do you think Olga feels?
5. Did Olga drink any milk today? Did she take vitamins?
6. Why does Mike care about what Olga eats?
7. What will Mike do to help?
8. Do you think it's important to eat well? Why or why not?
9. Do men cook or go shopping in your native country?
10. What did you have for supper yesterday? Who cooked it?

Working Together

Pregnant women aren't the only people who need balanced diets. Nutritionists say that everyone should eat at least one selection each day from each of the four major food groups:

Milk and milk products	Meat, fish, poultry, and eggs
Fruits and vegetables	Cereals and whole grains

Work with a partner. Person A asks about foods from the list below (and other foods that he or she thinks of). Person B answers, indicating which food group the item falls into.

> apples, corn, yogurt, ice cream, spinach, chicken, bread, rice, oranges, bananas, lamb chops, hamburger, bun, cottage cheese, oatmeal, butter, steak, celery, tomatoes, potatoes, tuna, skim milk, eggs, turkey, rolls

Real Talk

Sometimes a *yes/no* question is asked in statement form.

Example: *That's it?*

You can tell it is a question because the voice rises at the end of the sentence and it is written with a question mark. This form is used mostly in informal conversation, to express surprise.

■ ■ ■ ■ ■ Putting It Together

Many/Much

Use *many* with countable nouns:
There are **many** vitamins in oranges.

Countable nouns: oranges, potatoes, doctors, people, dollars.

Use *much* with noncountable nouns:
There is too **much** fat in butter.

Noncountable nouns: butter, oil, coffee, milk, sugar, rice, money.

Practice A

Complete each question below using *much* or *many*. Work in pairs. Person A asks the question, and Person B answers. Guess if you don't know the answer. Then switch roles.

1. A: How _____ milk should a child drink every day?
   B: _____

2. A: Do you eat _____ vegetables?
   B: _____

3. A: How _____ eggs are in a dozen?
   B: _____

4. A: Do you drink _____ coffee?
   B: _____

5. A: Do you think beef has too _____ fat?
   B: _____

6. A: How _____ apples did you eat yesterday?
   B: _____

Practice B

Work with a partner. Ask questions about the foods in the list on page 75. Ask *How much* or *How many* of an item your partner eats per week.

Sample questions:
    How many oranges do you eat per week?
    How much skim milk do you drink per week?

Read the passage and try to guess the meaning of the underlined words. Rephrase each paragraph. Then answer the questions below.

Checking the Ingredients

In the U.S., labels on food packages must give <u>nutritional</u> information about the product. The <u>ingredients</u> must be listed in order of weight. This list allows you to compare the contents of different brands and to tell which foods have too much sugar or salt (sodium), for example. You can also tell if there are dangerous <u>additives</u>.

Many food labels show exactly how much <u>protein</u>, fat, and <u>calories</u> are in one serving of the product. They also give information about <u>nutrients</u>, such as Vitamin C, iron, and calcium. The federal government has a <u>recommended</u> <u>daily</u> <u>allowance</u> (RDA) for most nutrients. Food labels must tell what percentage of the RDA one <u>serving</u> of the food provides.

However, some foods do not have labels, or they have additives that aren't on the label. For instance, many farmers feed <u>hormones</u> and <u>antibiotics</u> to farm animals, so our milk, eggs, and meat may contain these additives. Farmers usually spray plants with <u>insecticides</u>; shippers may spray fruits and vegetables with <u>preservatives</u> or wax. It is always wise to wash <u>produce</u> before you eat it.

1. What must be listed on food packages?
2. What does "RDA" mean?
3. What dangerous substances may be in milk and meat products?
4. What dangerous substances may be on fruits and vegetables?
5. How can you avoid additives, insecticides, and preservatives?

In Your Community

Find out the information individually or in groups and share it with the class.

1. Bring in nutritional information labels from cereals, breads, frozen or canned goods, and food products. Compare the amounts of protein, fat, calories, fiber, and vitamins.
2. Keep track of the food you eat for a week. Do you eat foods from the four basic food groups each day?
3. Get a nutritional chart from the library. Use the chart to compare the food values of the following: baked potatoes and french fried potatoes, butter and vegetable oil, four ounces of hamburger and four ounces of tofu.

■■■■■ Figuring Out the U.S.

As you read the passage below, circle the words you don't understand and try to guess their meanings.

Dieting

Movies and advertising tell Americans that "thin is beautiful." Doctors warn about health dangers of being overweight. Many Americans go on diets to look more like movie and TV stars or to feel better. They may eat less and stop eating desserts and sweets.

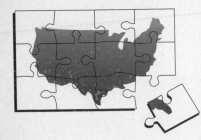

Helping people lose weight is big business in the U.S. There are diet clubs that have weekly lectures and group "weigh-ins" to help people stay on diets. Drug stores sell many brands of liquid or powdered diet aids. Soft drinks with artificial sweeteners and many brands of low-calorie foods are sold everywhere. Magazines contain the latest "fad" diets—special combinations of food designed to make people lose weight fast.

Often, a weight problem gets worse after a person tries to diet. Within a year, 95 percent of all dieters gain back more pounds than they lost. Only 5 percent of dieters are successful in staying thinner. Their secret is that they lose weight slowly, exercise regularly, and get and keep good eating habits.

Your Turn

Discuss the questions.

1. In the U.S., what pressures make people want to be thin? What are some examples of these pressures?
2. In your native country, do people worry about being overweight?
3. What is the basic diet of people in your native country? Do you feel that this is a healthy diet?
4. Have your eating habits changed since you came to the United States? If so, how?
5. Do you want to improve your eating habits? Why or why not? Are there any foods that you avoid? Why?

> *Choose one of the questions and write about it.*

■■■■■ Review Unit Four

Person A

Work with a partner. Look at this page only, and your partner will look at page 80 only.

The chart below gives nutritional information for 8 ounces of a cola drink and 8 ounces of orange juice. Some of the information on this chart is missing. Ask for the information and write it in. Use questions like these:

How many calories does the orange juice have?
How much protein does the cola drink have?

When you have completed the chart, take turns comparing the two drinks. Use the words *more* and *less*.

Example: *The cola has less niacin than the orange juice.*

	Cola drink	Orange juice
Calories	108	_____
Protein (grams)	_____	1.7
Carbohydrates (grams)	25.0	25.8
Fat (grams)	0.0	0.5
Cholesterol (milligrams)	0.0	0.0
Fiber (grams)	0.0	0.3
Caffeine (milligrams)	_____	0.0
Vitamin A (I.U.)	0.0	_____
C (milligrams)	0.0	74
D (I.U.)	0.0	0.0
E (milligrams)	0.0	0.1
B_1 (milligrams)	0.0	0.2
B_2 (milligrams)	0.0	0.1
Niacin (milligrams)	0.0	1.0
B_6 (milligrams)	0.0	0.1
Calcium (milligrams)	0.0	_____
Potassium (milligrams)	_____	496
Iron (milligrams)	0.0	0.5

Person B

Work with a partner. Look at this page only, and your partner will look at page 79 only.

The chart below gives nutritional information for 8 ounces of a cola drink and 8 ounces of orange juice. Some of the information on this chart is missing. Ask for the information and write it in. Use questions like these:

How many calories does the cola drink have?
How much caffeine does the orange juice have?

When you have completed the chart, take turns comparing the two drinks. Use the words *more* and *less*.

Example: *The cola has less niacin than the orange juice.*

	Cola drink	Orange juice
Calories	_____	111
Protein (grams)	0.0	1.7
Carbohydrates (grams)	_____	25.8
Fat (grams)	0.0	0.5
Cholesterol (milligrams)	0.0	0.0
Fiber (grams)	0.0	0.3
Caffeine (milligrams)	30.7	_____
Vitamin A (I.U.)	_____	496
C (milligrams)	0.0	_____
D (I.U.)	0.0	0.0
E (milligrams)	0.0	0.1
B_1 (milligrams)	0.0	0.2
B_2 (milligrams)	0.0	0.1
Niacin (milligrams)	0.0	1.0
B_6 (milligrams)	0.0	0.1
Calcium (milligrams)	0.0	27.0
Potassium (milligrams)	0.0	_____
Iron (milligrams)	0.0	0.5

Appendix

The Body

1. face
2. mouth
3. neck
4. shoulder
5. arm
6. elbow
7. wrist
8. armpit
9. back
10. chest
11. waist
12. abdomen
13. buttocks
14. hip
15. leg
16. thigh
17. knee
18. calf
19. ankle

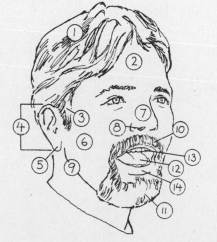

The Head

1. hair
2. forehead
3. sideburn
4. ear
5. earlobe
6. cheek
7. nose
8. nostril
9. jaw
10. moustache
11. beard
12. tongue
13. tooth (teeth)
14. lip
15. eye
16. eyebrow
17. eyelid
18. eyelashes

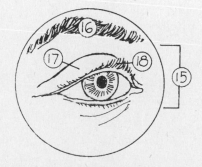

The Hand

1. fingernail
2. thumb
3. index finger
4. middle finger
5. ring finger
6. little finger
7. palm
8. knuckle

The Foot (feet)

1. heel
2. instep (arch)
3. ball
4. toe
5. big toe
6. little toe
7. toenail

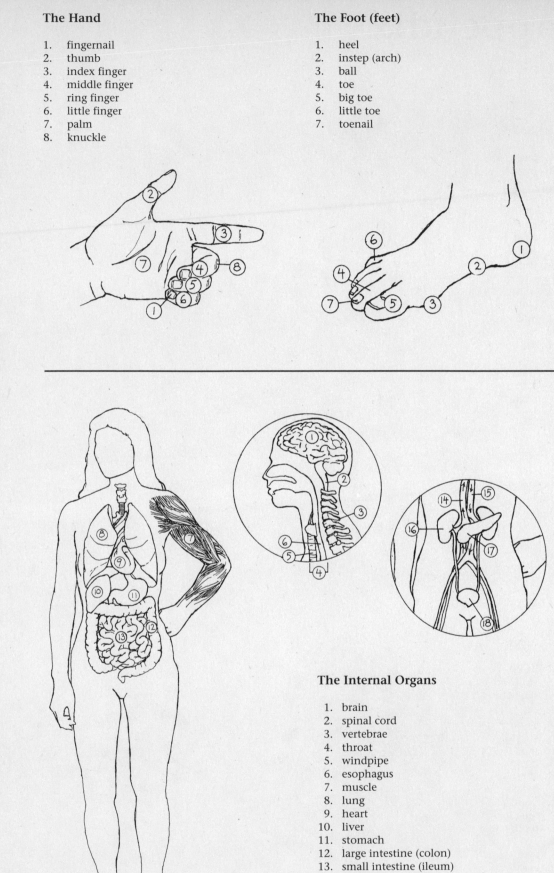

The Internal Organs

1. brain
2. spinal cord
3. vertebrae
4. throat
5. windpipe
6. esophagus
7. muscle
8. lung
9. heart
10. liver
11. stomach
12. large intestine (colon)
13. small intestine (ileum)
14. vein
15. artery
16. kidney
17. pancreas
18. bladder

■■■■■ Irregular Verbs in *In Good Health*

Basic Form	Simple Past	Past Participle
become	became	become
begin	began	begun
bleed	bled	bled
break	broke	broken
buy	bought	bought
catch	caught	caught
choose	chose	chosen
come	came	come
cost	cost	cost
do	did	done
draw	drew	drawn
drink	drank	drunk
drive	drove	driven
eat	ate	eaten
fall	fell	fallen
feed	fed	fed
feel	felt	felt
find	found	found
get	got	gotten (got)
give	gave	given
go	went	gone
have	had	had
hear	heard	heard
hit	hit	hit
hold	held	held
hurt	hurt	hurt
keep	kept	kept
know	knew	known
let	let	let
lie	lay	lain
lose	lost	lost
make	made	made
meet	met	met
pay	paid	paid
put	put	put
quit	quit	quit
read	read	read
ride	rode	ridden
run	ran	run
say	said	said

Basic Form	Simple Past	Past Participle
see	saw	seen
sell	sold	sold
send	sent	sent
shake	shook	shaken
sit	sat	sat
sleep	slept	slept
speak	spoke	spoken
spend	spent	spent
spread	spread	spread
stand	stood	stood
stick	stuck	stuck
take	took	taken
teach	taught	taught
tell	told	told
think	thought	thought
understand	understood	understood
wear	wore	worn
write	wrote	written

Temperature Conversion Table

Centigrade (Celsius)	Fahrenheit
36	96.8
36.1	97
36.6	98
37	98.6 →(Normal human body temperature,
37.2	99 plus or minus 1 degree)
37.7	100 → mild fever
38	100.4
38.3	101
39	102.2
39.4	103 → serious fever
40	104
40.5	105 → dangerous fever
41	105.8

◼◼◼◼◼ Index

The following is a list of the words and phrases found in the Words to Know and Another Way to Say It sections.